moment
meditations

Love Binds Us Together

Stormie Omartian

Harvest House Publishers
Eugene, Oregon

Love Binds Us Together

Copyright © 2000 by Stormie Omartian
Published by Harvest House Publishers, Eugene, Oregon 97402

ISBN 0-7369-0193-0

Text is adapted from *That's What Love Is For* by Stormie Omartian
(Harvest House Publishers, 1998).

Design and production by Left Coast Design, Portland, Oregon
Artwork by Gwendolyn Babbitt

Harvest House Publishers has made every effort to trace the ownership
of all poems and quotes. In the event of a question arising from the use of
a poem or quote, we regret any error made and will be pleased to make
the necessary correction in future editions of this book.

Printed in China.

00 01 02 03 04 05 06 07 08 09 / PP / 10 9 8 7 6 5 4 3 2 1

*L*ove smoothes the rough edges of our lives and gives us the strength to keep going forward. Love reminds us that when all seems lost, it can change everything for the best. Love is strong, selfless, unwavering, and unconditional. Love fills us with joy, grows us up, carries us through, strengthens our hearts, and gives us hope. Love is life changing. God is love, and through relationship with Him we can experience all the love He has for us.

The fruit of
the Spirit is
love,

joy,

peace,

patience,

kindness,

goodness,

faithfulness,

gentleness,

self-control.

GALATIANS

5:22,23

Gwendolyn Babbitt
© 1987

ove is a sacrifice, a loyal heart, a warm
smile, a generous spirit, a choice we make,
an encouraging word, an expression of
kindness.

Small things done in great love bring joy.

MOTHER TERESA

Remember each day you are loved by God, and that will enable you to give love away. Those who have been loved greatly see opportunities to love everywhere, in everything. It is easy to give love when we have been loved. Receive His great love for you now, and you will be able to pour it out on others.

We love, because He first loved us.

1 JOHN 4:19

Love seeks one thing only: the good of the one loved.
It leaves all other secondary effects to take care of
themselves. Love, therefore, is its own reward.

THOMAS MERTON

people who have ready smiles, kind words, and a genuine interest in those around them—what a wonderful pattern for our lives! These are the people who have love to give and are willing to give it without a thought of it being returned. Bind them close to your heart and don't ever let go.

Take note of those who live according to the pattern we gave you.

PHILIPPIANS 3:17 NIV

Even simple acts of love can be powerful. Though we don't always feel like it, each of us has something to give. The littlest act of love, done with a kind and patient heart, can be a wonderful and profound blessing.

That best portion of a man's life, his nameless, unremembered acts of kindness and love.

WILLIAM WORDSWORTH

Love is patient, love is kind.

1 CORINTHIANS 13:4 NIV

*C*hicken soup and a little care are always a good idea when someone around you is not feeling their best, but there is nothing like love to brighten their eyes. Tell them as well as show them that you love them. Love is truly the best medicine.

We were gentle among you, like a mother caring for her little children.

1 THESSALONIANS 2:7 NIV

We reap what we sow. Love has an amazing law of return. If we give love, it will come back to us. And there will always be a compensation far greater than what we have given, even though we may need to wait a little to reap the full consequences.

Give, and it will be given to you; good measure, pressed down, shaken together, running over, they will pour into your lap.

LUKE 6:38

KEYS

Love each other
with brotherly
affection and
take delight
in honoring
each other.

ROMANS
12:10 TLB

Gwendolyn Babbitt
© 1987

*L*ove blossoms when we reach out in acceptance of others, thinking the best of them, believing in them, and putting their needs before our own. Faithfully watch over the garden of your heart. Weed it carefully and often so that love can grow.

Love is a fruit in season at all times,
and within the reach of every hand.

MOTHER TERESA

*W*hen it becomes hard to love another person, pray for them. Before you know it, you'll be able to see them through God's eyes and His love will overflow in your heart.

❧

Beloved, let us love one another,
for love is from God.

1 JOHN 4:7

When we invite the love of God to fill our hearts, it crowds out negative emotions so completely that we are free to love others at a depth we would otherwise never know.

Let your heart therefore be wholly devoted to the LORD our God.

1 KINGS 8:60

Pursue righteousness, godliness, faith, love, perseverance, and gentleness.

1 TIMOTHY
6:11

Gwendolyn Babbitt

*L*ove and negative emotions,
like envy, have two things in
common. They both require
effort, and they both can turn
into something big! Sometimes
the greatest act of love is simply to
resist that which would destroy it.

ༀ

*Every day should be distinguished by
at least one particular act of love.*

JOHANN KASPAR LAVATER

Acts of selfless love can be a little scary at times, but they also can be catalysts of great blessing. Restoration of broken relationships is often made possible because one party chose not to think of self, but instead chose to willingly love the other.

Love each other as
I have loved you.

JOHN 15:12 NIV

Love is keeping a promise, knowing when to let go, rejoicing with those who rejoice, believing for the best in someone, accepting others for who they really are, taking time to really know a person, making a sacrifice only you can possibly make.

Love . . . bears all things, believes all things, hopes all things, endures all things.

1 CORINTHIANS 13:7

Greater love has no one than this,
than to lay down one's life for his friends.

JOHN 15:13 NKJV

When we love, we no longer need to prove we are right. And even if we are right, sometimes the more loving thing to do is to humble ourselves and let the other person win. More often than not, acts of selfless love make everyone feel like a winner.

Gentle feelings produce profoundly beneficial effects upon stern natures. It is the spring rain which melts the ice-covering of the earth, and it causes it to open to the beams of heaven.

FREDRIKA BREMER

Humility enables us to work through our differences. When we respond humbly to another person, it makes them feel loved and valued. Humility can break down the walls built up between us and help bind us together.

Be completely humble and gentle; be
patient, bearing with one another in love.

EPHESIANS 4:2 NIV

Do nothing from selfishness...but with humility of mind let each of you regard one another as more important than himself.

PHILIPPIANS 2:3

Working through the complexities of relationships can sometimes be hard, but if we are willing to be flexible and forgiving, and diligent to sow seeds of understanding, those close to us will always feel loved.

Love is an act of endless forgiveness...
PETER USTINOV

With little ones around, sometimes an expression of love is letting them help you even when you can do it better by yourself. It is an act of humble and sacrificial love to deliberately include others in our lives.

You should be like one big happy family. . .loving one another with tender hearts and humble minds.

1 PETER 3:8 TLB

*L*ove produces love. The more we love, the more we are capable of loving, and the more we will feel the love of others towards us. An act of love is like a stone falling into a lake. The ripple effect goes on and on…

ॐ

Love each other as I have loved you.

JOHN 15:12 NIV

*R*eaching out to touch a stranger is an act of love we can't afford not to offer. All it requires is a small gesture of compassion or a tender word that shows we are willing to give something of ourselves to bring happiness into another person's life.

❧

Today, see if you can stretch your heart and expand your love so that it touches not only those to whom you can give it easily, but also those who need it so much.

DAPHNE ROSE KINGMA

For I was hungry, and you gave Me something
to eat; I was thirsty, and you gave Me drink;
I was a stranger, and you invited Me in.

MATTHEW 25:35

*L*ove is not giving up, simply listening,
being transparent, bearing another's
burden, reaching out and touching,
giving with no thought of a return,
showing compassion for the suffering
of others.

*Bear one another's burdens, and
thus fulfill the law of Christ.*

GALATIANS 6:2

*L*ove makes us want whatever is best for another. When you love someone, you are aware of their discomfort and you do what is necessary to make them feel more comfortable. Love enables us to do things we never thought we could.

Don't think only of yourself. Try to think of the other...and what is best for him.

1 CORINTHIANS 10:24 TLB

LOVE DWELLS WITHIN

Gwendolyn
Babbitt ©

*W*hen we know God, we come face to face with a love so powerful it transforms our life, helps us rise above our frailties, and makes us better than we could ever hope to be on our own.

❧

All love is sweet, given or returned. They who inspire it most are fortunate...but those who feel it most are happiest still.

PERCY BYSSHE SHELLEY

Rosa
sp.

Gwendolyn Babbitt©

Therefore,
if anyone is
in Christ, he is
a new creation; old
things have passed
away; behold,
all things have
become new.

2 CORINTHIANS
5:17 NKJV

Be kind and
compassionate
to one another,
forgiving each other,
just as in Christ
God forgave you.

EPHESIANS 4:32

NIV

*L*ove is not keeping score, not passing judgment, forgiving over and over, not taking things personally, giving the benefit of the doubt, not doing it again after you apologize, taking someone's past into consideration.

*L*ove can change a life, a nation, or the world. Our sphere of influence may seem small in our own eyes; but a little love can produce large results. Why not give all the love and compassion you can right where you are? What better place to start changing the world?

Every time you smile at someone, it is an action of love, a gift to that person, a beautiful thing.

MOTHER TERESA

For the whole Law is fulfilled in one word... "you shall love your neighbor as yourself."

GALATIANS 5:14

*But a certain Samaritan. . . came upon
him; and when he saw him, he felt compassion,
and came to him, and bandaged up his wounds,
pouring oil and wine on them; and he put
him on his own beast, and brought him
to an inn, and took care of him.*

LUKE 10:33,34

*L*ove doesn't always have to be a great commitment of undying devotion. It can be a simple moment of compassion for another human being. A single act of love can have far-reaching effects.

When our words are laced with forgiveness, kindness, mercy, and love, they can make a wonderful difference in someone's day. Long after loving words cease to be heard by the ear, their message resonates loudly in the heart.

Pleasant words are a honeycomb, sweet to the soul and healing to the bones.

PROVERBS 16:24

Kindness is the insignia of a loving heart.
E.C. McKenzie

*L*ove comforts, is more than a feeling, means being responsible, gives us a vision for the future, shows mercy instead of judgment, and is the foundation for all lasting change.

જી

"For I know the thoughts that I think toward you," says the LORD, "thoughts of peace and not evil to give you a future and a hope."

JEREMIAH 29:11 NKJV

here is no greater feeling than that of knowing we are loved. It enables us to fly, to soar on top of the world, to endure anything. It is the source of all joy.

God has put something noble and good into every heart which His hand created.

MARK TWAIN

The LORD appeared to him...
saying, "I have loved you with
an everlasting love; therefore
I have drawn you with
lovingkindness."

JEREMIAH 31:3

*L*ove brings us joy, clears our minds, gives us courage, fills us with hope, lights up our darkness, strengthens our hearts, lifts us to heights we've never imagined.

❧

The LORD your God is in your midst...
He will rejoice over you with gladness,
He will quiet you with His love, He
will rejoice over you with singing.

ZEPHANIAH 3:17 NKJV

*L*ove and prayer naturally go together. Pray for those dear to you that the love of God will bless them today. Pray that when opportunities come to show love, you will be aware of them and quick to respond.

૭

Never miss a chance to love when it is offered.
What you get back will sustain you forever.

CHRISTOPHER REEVES

We give thanks to God... praying always for you.

COLOSSIANS 1:3

he only love that never fails is God's love. And though we are human, there is one foolproof act of love that always works—the act of praying. When we want to show someone unfailing love, prayer is the way to start.

⁓

I thank my God in all my remembrance
of you, always offering prayer with
joy in my every prayer for you all.
PHILIPPIANS 1:3,4

he love we give in a day will multiply far beyond what we could ever imagine. It will flow through the lives we touch into the lives they touch, and on and on love will go—serving, healing, saving, forgiving, sustaining, and transforming.

Love never fails.

1 CORINTHIANS 13:8